# Sport Trucks

## Custom Cool

Pat Kytola and Larry Kytola

First published in 1989 by Motorbooks International Publishers & Wholesalers, P O Box 2, 729 Prospect Avenue, Osceola, WI 54020 USA



Printed and bound in Singapore



**Library of Congress Cataloging-in-Publication Data**

Kytola, Pat

Sport trucks / Pat Kytola, Larry Kytola.

p. cm.

ISBN 0-87938-366-6

1. Trucks—Customizing. I. Kytola, Larry. II. Title.

TL230.K97 1989 89-9265

629.28'73—dc20 CIP

Motorbooks International books are also available at discounts in bulk quantity for industrial or sales-promotional use. For details write to Special Sales Manager at the Publisher's address

**On the front cover:** *Kevin and Pamela McCarthy of Tucson, Arizona, left the factory red paint on their 1987 Toyota, then applied a coat of hand-mixed blue paint over the top to achieve these superb graphics. This truck is first class all around—boasting even a dash-mounted television.*

**On the back cover:** Daddy's Girl, *a real car crusher, is owned and operated by a seventeen-year-old girl, Michelle Ely. The truck was built by her father, Sonny Ely, and his partner Sam Sturges. It is a Chevrolet S-10 equipped with an alcohol-injected 454 ci engine mated to a 400 transmission; the engine is located in the rear. Other modifications include sport bars with the lights mounted on top, lots of chrome panels and, of course, the tracks, which are off of an Army personnel carrier but work well to get the traction needed for crushing and pulling contests.*

**On the frontispiece:** *Sport trucks come in all shapes and sizes. This remote-control truck,* Big Brute, *was built from a model kit by Kyle Roth of Tucson. The model is an exact replica of Roth's 1984 Toyota four-wheel-drive sport truck. It took Roth only ten hours to complete the model, but he says it draws more attention than the full-size version that took hundreds of hours to complete.*

**On this page:** *With the help of some friends, Jesus Robles of Tucson built this 1978 GMC Sierra Classic painted pearl-brown with graphics. In this picture it appears that the box has been removed, but it actually has a scissor bed that tilts; it is shown up in the air.*

# Birth of sport trucking

When pickups first appeared on the market they were constructed strictly for practical purposes, and were used mainly for farm work or for hauling heavy objects. In the seventies, the buying public began to realize these trucks could also be used for play. Truck manufacturers heeded this trend and went back to the drawing board to design the type of vehicle the public wanted. They designed a pickup with two- and four-wheel drive, and added a new type of enclosed body design to their line-up of workhorses. But styles have changed, giving birth to the sport truck. Sport truck owners began with the basic model the manufacturer produced, and with lots of imagination and creative ability along with some hard-earned dollars, added features and subtracted inches to build their trucks. Manufacturers are watching this latest trend carefully. They have come a long way in what they offer the public.

Jeep implemented aerodynamics when they restyled the sheet metal for the new year's sport truck. The headlights, bumpers and sideglass will be more streamlined. Dodge also has implemented aerodynamics into their latest models, and will be offering a V-8 engine in the next year's line-up. Another sporty feature Dodge is offering the truck-buying public is the Dodge Dakota convertible truck. Look for it to appear in 1989. Carroll Shelby has even become involved in this new sport, taking the Dodge Dakota and adding a 5.2 liter, 318 ci V-8 engine. Other features include fender lips, a light bar, an air dam and, of course, the Shelby emblems.

Mazda has also been watching the whims of the American sport trucking scene and has joined Toyota and Mitsubishi in adding graphics to their trucks once they reach US shores. Mazda, with the help of 3M, has been studying the demographics of the potential buyer. Using this information, the graphics are produced and applied once the trucks are dockside, allowing Mazda to tailor the trucks to whatever area of the country they are destined for.

So no matter what your creativity or artistic ability, you should be able to find or build a sport truck to meet your dreams.

**Previous page**

*When some people think of sport trucks they limit the years to the late seventies and the eighties, but at the March 1989 Sport Truck Nationals in Tucson, I spotted this 1940 Ford truck. Is it a street rod or a sport truck? How about both! The truck, owned by Micky and Sue Hunt of Mesa, Arizona, is painted 1957 GM fleet green with reverse graphics of candy purple paint from the House of Kolor. Micky chose to modify the body by chopping the top three inches. The engine and drivetrain have been changed to include 1981 Corvette rear suspension with Mustang II front suspension. The unit is powered by the ever-dependable 350 ci small-block Chevrolet engine. Boyd wheels were used to dress up the exterior of this truck along with a polished chrome rear end. Micky used oak and walnut inlaid wood to make the bed. A leather tonneau cover protects the wood from the elements. Creature comforts consist of a Panasonic stereo system in the overhead console, all-leather upholstery, wool carpeting, air conditioning, power disc brakes front and rear, power antenna and a built-in radar detector.*

*This truck proves that the smaller-body styled trucks are not the only ones considered sport trucks. This big one-ton dually 1988 Chevrolet named* Picture Perfect, *belonging to Michael Balong, is a fine example of a sport truck of another version. The one-ton truck is powered by a 454 ci fuel-injected engine.*

*Custom Creations did a fantastic job on the upholstery for* Picture Perfect, *as you can see. The truck seats 11 people: five in the front and six in the rear. The captain's chairs in the front add to the comfort and luxury of the ride. Passengers can use the cellular telephone, watch the color television or listen to the Alpine AM/FM radio or CD tuner. There are 14 speakers and three amplifiers for the listeners' pleasure, and the table in the box comes in handy for several uses. The addition of the sun visor, chrome running boards, chrome wheels plus the topper from Desert Dynamics and the paint work by Signs & Stripes of Tucson make this one sharp-looking sport truck.*

*Sun, sand and surf is the theme.* Cabriolet for Play *is what Tony and Cher Salvemini of Tucson call their Euro-styled sport truck. Tony has spent many hours hand rubbing the bright red factory paint on this 1987 Mazda to bring out the high-luster shine. Signs & Stripes of Tucson are responsible for the superb job with the graphics and other paint detailing. The unique display that Tony set up near the truck instantly draws attention to his vehicle. Look closely from every angle in order to catch all the trick detailing features used to make this a winner. The HoTTops top conversion kit was installed by his friend Chris Klinger. Tony claims that his truck is the only one around that is at least 98 percent leak-proof due to Klinger's expertise.*

Cabriolet
FOR PLAY!
mazda
TONY & CHAR SALVEMINI
CHRIS KLINGER
TUCSON SEAT COVER
OWNER
SIGNS & STRIPES
MEN
CHROME

*The fine detailing of the* Cabriolet for Play *Mazda is carried over into the engine compartment. The air cleaner cover is painted to match the exterior of the truck, as are several other components.*

*Tony Salvemini lowered his truck six inches from stock height and proceeded to detail the undercarriage with striping and extensive use of chrome plating. The tire was removed to expose this fine detailing.*

*Salvemini chose Corbeau seats and hired Tucson Seat Covers to customize and modify the interior of his sport truck. He implemented a Formuling steering wheel, and makes the ride more enjoyable with the use of a JVC stereo system. The dash has been painted red to add to the Euro look.*

*Detailing stands out when you are looking at a sport truck, right down to the paint features added to the taillight lens. The same type of detailing can be found on the undercarriage of Salvemini's Mazda. Note also the paint detailing on the tailgate and box side.*

*Toyota would be amazed to see the volume of chrome that Frank Olguin of Nogales, Arizona, has added to his gray 1978 Land Cruiser. As a matter of fact, they would be totally amazed to see what else he has done to his vehicle. Olguin mastered everything himself except for the paint job. The Toyota is now equipped with an 8,000 pound winch for pulling capacity. Armstrong Norsemen 12½ inch radials are the tires that Olguin chose to be mated to his 15×10 inch American Outlaw Racing wheels. The dash is stock except for the addition of an amp gauge, a La Carra steering wheel was used in place of the stock one. The seats, also stock, are reupholstered with custom velour material. The only chrome that was stock on this vehicle at the time of manufacture was the chrome door latches. If you look closely here you will see that all these parts are chrome: the heater, headers, console, roll bars, grille, bumpers, air vents, gas filler door and back of the rear seats. Bushwacker fender flares add styling to the rear. One common practice of sport truckers is to add KC lights; Olguin did this, mounting them on the windshield. For better handling, Olguin chose to use a system of advanced handling suspension backed with Saginaw power steering and dual El Ranchero shocks.*

LAND CRUISER
ARMSTRONG
RADIAL

*One of the neatest features of Frank Olguin's Toyota Land Cruiser is the engine—look at all the chrome goodies. What else do you see? That's right, a Chevrolet engine. This Toyota has a Camaro 327 ci engine; Olguin is satisfied with the results that he achieved with this setup.*

Neon NANNA *is what Richard Swindle of Tucson has named his 1979 Chevrolet pickup. Swindle says that there is not one piece of this truck that has not been modified, and you better believe him! Look at the taillights—they are about the trickest things around. The red, blue and green neon stripes accenting the body lines on the rear of this truck add to its uniqueness.*

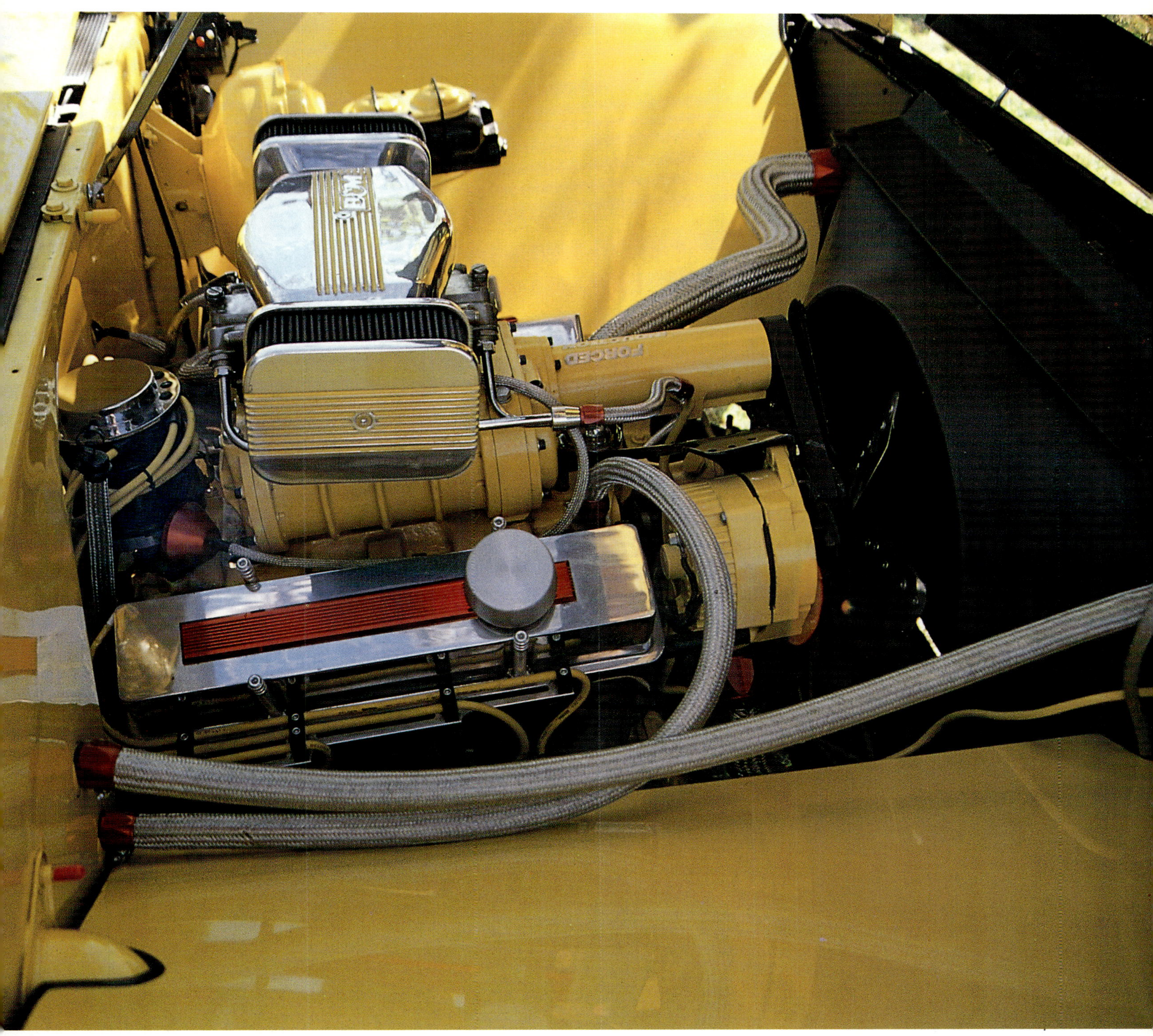


*Don't challenge Richard Swindle to a race by revving your engine at a stoplight or you may be left sitting in the dust. Under the hood of this truck is a 406 ci small-block supercharged Chevrolet engine. The suicide hood is equipped to work off gas struts, and the grille is handmade using 160 feet of solid stock.*

*A better shot of the graphics on this 1979 Chevrolet pickup, painted Corvette yellow, belonging to Richard Swindle. The colors accent the bright yellow on the body but the paint is not the only sharp-looking feature. The top has been chopped six inches, making the body appear better proportioned. The antenna has been Frenched-in, and door handles have been shaved and a remote switch molded in between the cab and the box. Swindle did all the work himself, except for the louvers and the glass. B. F. Goodrich radial tires wrap around the Enkei wheels, which have their centers painted yellow to match the body.*

*The sport truck market is developing rapidly, and it seems that almost everyone in Tucson who is involved is marketing a new product line. The company that owns this 1988 Mazda is called HoTTops of Tucson. HoTTops sells almost all your sport truck needs from wipers to tonneau covers, nose bras (as pictured here) to lowering blocks and blue dots. Even all the ground effects can be had from HoTTops. The nose bras come in many colors to match the colors sport truck fans have come to love—bright! If you like the convertible top you see on this Mazda, you can even purchase from HoTTops a conversion kit to get your sport truck lid replaced.*

*Graphics, sign painting and stripes are quite common on most sport trucks. Here is a fine example of the creativity that is being shown today. This design is on a 1988 Mazda owned by HoTTops, as you can see advertised on the cartoon character's T-shirt.*

*An 89 degree Fahrenheit March day in Tucson, with blue skies and white puffy clouds, the bright colors of the sport trucks and beautiful grounds of the Pima County fairgrounds. This display of trucks advertising for HoTTops could not have been parked in a better setting.*

HOTTOPS
AUTO
AUTO

Sweet Dreams *is the name of the sport truck of Danny O'Neill and Michele Gerard, and describes the truck well, right down to the display they have chosen to use around it. The sign lists all the people who have helped O'Neill complete the truck. Pink and blue are the colors used on the truck, even on the oil, gas and water cans, the first-aid kit and the toolbox. The toolbox is full of tools, but who knows if they are used or are just for display purposes?*

*Pink and blue on white is the theme on this truck: blue seats and door panels with pink trim, pink floor mats and pink door handles. The theme is so symmetrical that you will find one sideview mirror pink and one blue; the pink mirror has a blue housing and the blue mirror a pink housing. The engine also utilizes the pink and blue theme, using pink hoses, blue air cleaner and so on.*

NEWPORT
SURF&SPORT

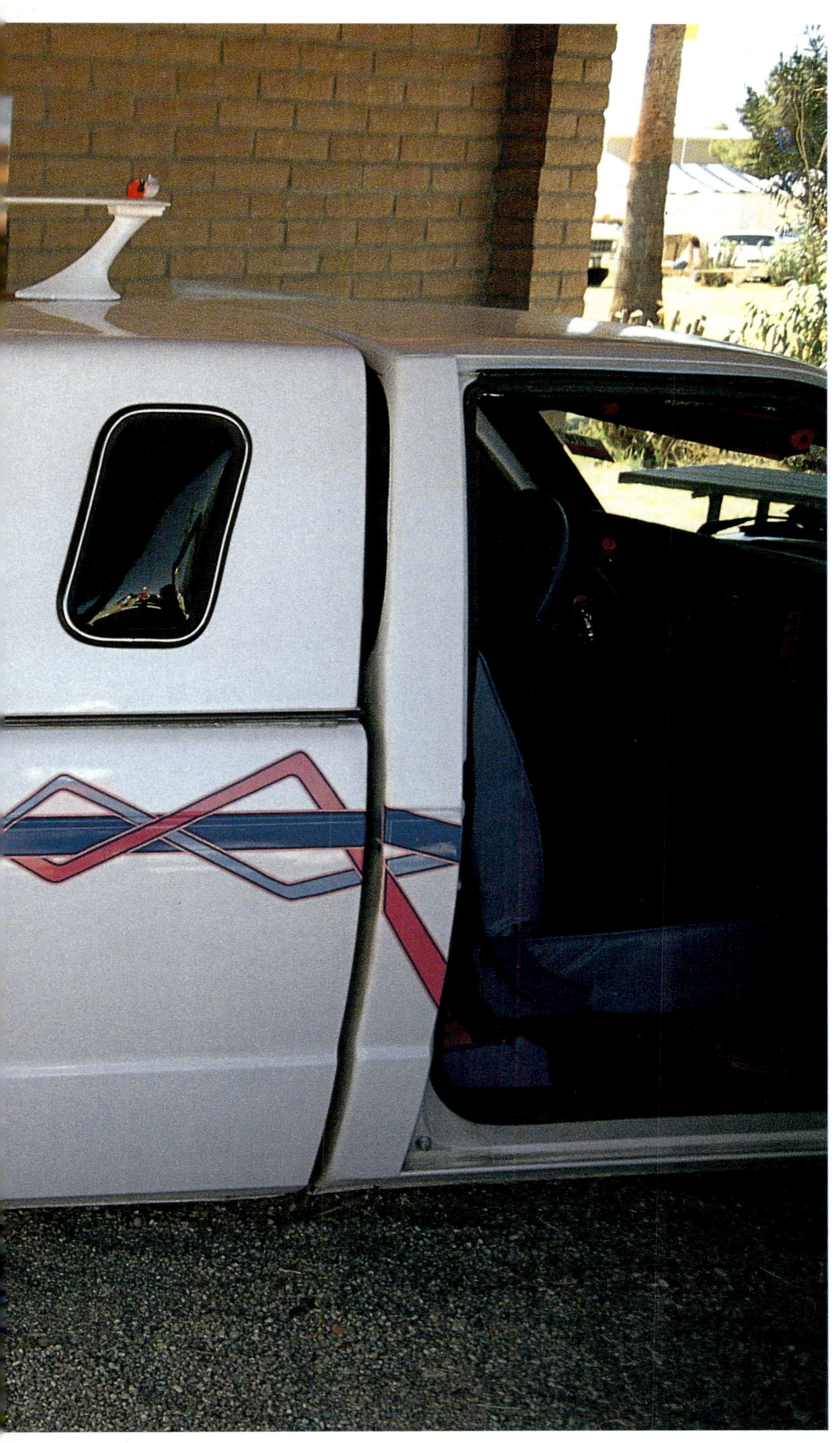

*Chevrolet has never had a truck as fully equipped as this one roll off their assembly line. This 1982 Chevrolet S-10 is painted white with pink and blue graphics, with the body and paint work completed by owner Danny O'Neill, except for the artwork and lettering which was done by Ray Signs of Tucson. You cannot see it in this picture, but all the lettering on the truck has been inverted. The bed of the truck is not meant to do any heavy hauling; it is carpeted, has a television set and VCR. Note the TV antenna on the camper built by Arizona Truck Outfitters. The stereo equipment is from Stereo Pad—and what a system it is! There are so many speakers and the volume is so loud that pennies can be bounced off the roof.*

*Wendy Weger of Tucson says that her red Toyota four-wheel-drive truck is still under construction and by next year she will have added a new interior and stereo system. It looks to me like she has already added quite a unique touch to her truck, with the addition of the chromed and sandblasted tailgate insert. She did all the work herself.*

*A blue Chevrolet Blazer with pink ribbon graphics and a pink top. The chrome wheels and shiny black tires add to the beauty of the truck. A fun vehicle to take out and cruise the sand dunes.*

HOST CLUB
0152
Pretty n Pink

REST ROOMS
Rockford Fosgate

**Previous page**

*The beds on these two trucks seem to be at a peculiar angle. What would cause this? The addition of hydraulic tilt bed kits! Some truck owners use a scissor lift on their trucks, some use a diamond tilt and some use a dump bed setup. The trucks pictured here are the winners of the bed dancing contest at the March 1989 Sport Truck Nationals in Tucson. The maroon truck, utilizing a diamond tilt setup, was first-place winner. The third-place winner was quite unique. The bed did not have hydraulics, but it did have two men in the bed and they were dancing to the music. Unusual, but they took home a trophy. Todd Kamrowski, of Sierra Vista, Arizona, is the owner of this metallic blue 1980 Toyota four-wheel-drive truck that took second place in the contest. Kamrowski hired Jonathon Stone to do the striping work on his Toyota. The dress-up chrome plating and pink striping and trim make this a sharp-looking truck. Forty-inch Monster Mudders on 15 inch rims adorn the four corners. He has spent more than $14,000 for modifications to this truck so far, but feels that it is worth it, and he isn't finished yet!*

*A king's ransom has been spent for the chrome additions to this 1980 Toyota owned by Todd Kamrowski. Just a few of the items that have been chrome plated are the hydraulic rams, driveshaft, custom shock mounts, traction mounts, dash, bumpers, grille and sport bars. The hot pink shock boots contrast with the chrome to make a bold statement.*

*Paint of various colors and forms is part of the new look in sport trucking today. Traditionally, paint designs have followed and accented the body lines of cars and trucks—not so on today's vehicles.* Blown out of Proportion *is the name Tom Goodwin has chosen for his 1979 Toyota four-wheel-drive truck. Goodwin had Showtime do the paint, Auto-Visuals did the stripes and lettering. The body of the truck is black, accented with blue, red and yellow graphics and pinstriping. The suspension is by Off Road Plus with the traction by Pro Tires and Wheels.*

*"The wilder, the better" seems to be the message of today's sport trucks when it comes to painting. Signs & Stripes of Tucson appears to be doing a booming business with the sport truck market. This is another example of a superbly customized vehicle. Mark Jacob of Tucson is the owner. Note the striped taillight—this also seems to be a new trend.*

*A different graphic method, a splash of paint, was used on this blue Nissan. The chrome wheels, ground effects, top conversion and the silver, blue and orange paint combination make this truck a real classy ride.*

ORION

**Previous page**

*Another enterprising family that have taken their love for sport trucking and turned it into a profitable business, the John Pazos family of Tucson. Pazos advertises ragtops, ground effects and custom convertibles on his business cards. He is a distributor for both Soft Gate Sun Roofs and Radical Tops. The blue 1982 S–15 GMC, with the yellow and green graphics, is a fine example of the Pazos' workmanship. The GMC is adorned with B. F. Goodrich tires and Center Line Convo Pro wheels. The engine remains a stock V-6. The door handles have been shaved and replaced with electric push-button, pop-open doors with a concealed switch. The truck is equipped for sound with a CD disc player and speakers to accommodate the setup.*

*Another picture of John Pazos' 1982 S–15 GMC Sierra. The ground effects that are on the market today are made to fit the short-bed trucks, but Pazos chose to modify a set to fit his long-bed vehicle. His business, JJ & R Custom Conversions, did all the work on this truck including the bed and insert. The teddy bears add to the eye appeal. The seats are standard with custom upholstery.*

*The tailgate of John Pazos' S-15 GMC utilizes paint and design to advertise that this really is a business truck, not just a pleasure vehicle. You have to look closely at any of these trucks to catch all the details. The taillights on a stock S-15 GMC are located in the corners of the truck box, but notice that Pazos has moved them down to where the bumper normally is. Nice customizing idea.*

CONVERSION
AZOS
AZ89

*Suzuki Samurai fever has hit with a passion because of the low sticker price and individuality available straight from the dealer. Stability has proven to be a problem, but by lowering and customizing, as David Woodruff of Tucson has done with the three-inch D-arched springs and lowering kit, this problem has been alleviated. Utilizing ten-inch-wide KMC wheels gives greater command and driveability. The only thing that is stock here is the engine. The custom Safari top is a kit from Hard Tops of California. The sound system has a Sound Stream tape deck with Alpine amps, and audio speakers with two 12 inch speakers in the rear.*

0305
samurai

*Eddie Salcido of Tucson used a striking color combination on the exterior of his 1979 Chevy Blazer, combining a base coat of turquoise with graphics in magenta toner done by Randy Jensen and striped by Jim Gere in peach and mint green. Salcido is the owner and operator of Master Craft Auto Interiors in Tucson. He applied his professional skills to create the striking interior, with Cerullo front sport seats and handmade plywood rear seat, upholstered in aircraft turquoise tweed and Naugahyde. Interior bolt-on extras include a stereo from Classic Car Sounds and a Faz Gate Punch CD with Alpine speakers. Exterior modifications include molded bumper, filled tailgate and louvered hood—in a slightly different inverted version. The taillights are Lincoln Continental sidemarkers molded into the rear bumper. Valve covers and air cleaners are custom made by Jim Bich, and a 350 ci Chevy small-block mated to a Turbo 400 automatic transmission powers this rig. Quite a sporty unit.*

0117

Robert Rosso of Tucson owned this 1989 Isuzu for only four weeks. Unable to find a nitrous system that would fit his truck, Rosso purchased the unit designed for a 924 Porsche and modified it to fit his truck. The control switch is from a jet airplane. When he hits the nitrous oxide switch, he claims the truck goes from 45 to 85 mph almost instantaneously.

*This 1989 Isuzu appears as basically a stock truck. Signs & Stripes of Tucson did the artwork. The stock stereo system was stolen from Rosso's truck the night before these pictures were taken. B. F. Goodrich T A radials are stretched to fit on nine-inch KMC chrome wheels.*

Hi-Risk *is the name chosen for this orange 1971 Ford Bronco owned by Greg and Yolanda Leyba. Interior work was completed by Master Craft Auto Interiors. The aluminum louvered dash was custom made by Steve Davis of California. Comfort is the name of the game, whether driving on road or off.*

*The use of aluminum louvers can be found not only in the interior dash panels but also in the engine compartment of the 1971 Ford Bronco owned by Greg Leyba. The engine is a 351 Windsor mounted with plenty of chrome goodies. The four-speed transmission makes negotiating the backroads a joy.*

FORD
71 FORD
BRONCO 4X4
"HI RISK"

*Here's a look at Greg Leyba's entire vehicle. The bright orange exterior was painted by Paint 'N Place, and pinstriping was done by Jim Gere.*

**Previous page**

*Mike Clark, a native of Owensboro, Kentucky, is the proud owner of this red 1987 Nissan. Exterior paint is a base coat of red, with yellow, green and blue graphics done by Signs & Stripes. The vehicle is a sure show winner; the trophy by its side attests to this fact. Clark chose to use air shocks in place of hydraulics to raise and lower the bed. The engine is a stock four-cylinder. Clark says the truck is still not complete, and is continually devising minor detailing changes to implement.*

*Who spilled the paint on this red 1987 Nissan sport truck? Signs & Stripes of Tucson neatly splashed pink, orange, yellow, green, blue and purple paint down the door of this prize winner owned by Mike Clark. The splashes set the theme for the brightly colored graphics which add the finishing touches to this truck.*

*Wow—what an interior! The plush gray velour interior accented with red vinyl has multiple-colored stripes for a unique, eye-catching appearance. This interior was created by Custom Creations and installed in the 1987 Nissan owned by Mike Clark.*

*All that glitters is not gold, but may also be chrome, as seen here. Springs, wheels, struts, tailpipes, door panels, the undercarriage, running boards and the differential are all chrome. This 1960 Chevy, named* Baby Blue, *is owned by Pedro Escudero of Arizona.*

*Pedro Escudero has spent many affectionate hours of labor doing the interior, painting and chrome plating his 1960 Chevy* Baby Blue. *Note the roller-chain steering wheel. Individual features such as this make the whole truck unique. The interior door panels are inset with chrome plating, making for a mirror reflection of the rest of the truck. Custom taillights in the shape of an iron cross, with a blue dot in the center, replace the standard taillights.*

CHUVY 1
JR
CHUVY

**Previous page**

*Jesus Robles of Tucson owns this classic sport truck. He started out with a 1978 GMC Sierra Classic, adding such modifications as a 454 ci big-block Chevrolet engine, an electrifying stereo system installed in the box complete with a lighting system, power rear windows, sport bars with lights, an eight-inch lift kit, scissor and tilt bed, chrome louvers in the tailgate, 18 inch Centerline wheel complete with Mickey Thompson Baja tires and air deflectors over the side windows. Robles used a pearl-brown paint with graphics, creating a clean street appearance.*

*Who says sport trucks can't be comfortable? This plush interior is quite inviting. The custom interior was crafted by Speed Auto Seatcovers. Truck owner Pat Tarantino of Tucson likes his luxury, and with these seats he certainly has comfort.*

RADIAL LT

*An exterior picture of Pat Tarantino's 1980 Toyota. The Toyota 4×4 has a stock drivetrain and engine but does not look like a truck that came off the showroom floor. The truck was custom painted by Czechs Kustom Touch with five base colors, three of which are candy, fading from gold to root beer. The door handles have been shaved and filled, and a molded tailgate, custom top, dual shocks and molded visors are all modifications that Tarantino felt would add to the luxury of his vehicle.*

*Some friends from south of the border also came to enjoy the Sport Truck Spectacular in Tucson in March of 1989. Mario Mendival and his son, Mario, of Nogales, Sonora, Mexico, drove their 1982 Chevrolet S-10 to participate in this event. Like so many other people involved in sport trucks, they have made their hobby into a business, owning and operating Auto Serdico Mendivals in Nogales. They did all the work on the Chevy, including the custom graphics, tonneau cover and blue velour upholstery. The base coat of navy is accented with six candy colors ranging from apple red to purple to dark blue to royal blue to black and then to silver.*

CHEVROL
843 YYB

*A close-up of the tailgate of the S–10 belonging to Mario Mendival shows the outstanding artistry used. The paint job is one of the nicest around.*

*The Bell Tech Attack—that's the phrase being used to refer to the new look that Jim Ewing and Bell Tech have achieved. Super Bell Axle Company, a subsidiary of Bell Tech, has been into the hot-rod scene for years. They had the foresight to realize that the sport truck showed hot-rod potential. If you wish to achieve the lowered effect on your sport truck, you can install the dropped front spindle that they manufacture. They have worked closely with General Motors to create a spindle that lowers the vehicle and improves the handling, and still maintains the original ride quality. These suspension parts are designed with ease of installation in mind, which makes replacement more convenient. The white GMC in the foreground is Bell Tech's project truck. It is equipped with a Corvette engine and Corvette rear end, and has a rear roll pan which replaces the stock bumpers. The red crew cab in the background is also a Bell Tech truck, with the Euro tech styling and state-of-the-art equipment. Bell Tech also sells appearance items such as rear roll pans, bumper masks, aero mirrors, rear spring hangers and shackles, coils, lowering kits and many more items to make your sport truck just the way you want it.*

*Bell Tech has chosen white for the base color of their project GMC truck, with just a small amount of detail paint to accent the appearance. The light blue and pink striping are just the right touch.*

*This 1986½ Nissan Hardbody, owned by Rusty and Alisa Williamson of Tucson, is a daily driver. Signs & Stripes did another terrific paint job using Bunny Pink Wave, Candy Nile, Green Ooze and Turquoise Blue over a white background to achieve this unique look.*

0126

*A picture of the box and shell of Rusty and Alisa Williamson's 1986½ Nissan. The shell is from Arizona Truck Outfitters. Even in a family vehicle, the sound system is an important addition. They chose an Alpine stereo with CD player from Alpine Electronics. The bed is equipped so that it will tilt on command.*

*This 1987 red and blue Toyota truck belongs to Kevin and Pamela McCarthy of Tucson. The truck has been lowered eight inches below stock, and Keystone Classic Wheels with Bridgestone Potenza radial tires were used for ride stability and comfort. The undercarriage has been prepared for show and the truck has been fully carpeted, with all work being done by the owners. Added creature comforts consist of a Sony tape deck stereo, two stick amps and Pioneer speakers with MTX woofers. The dash is custom striped and is optionally equipped with a television set.*

TOYOTA
WILDCATS

*In the back of the truck you will see a custom bed liner and tail-mounted spoiler, features that add to the appearance of the McCarthy's 1987 Toyota.*

*All dressed up in red and blue, this 1987 Toyota sport truck is owned by Kevin and Pamela McCarthy. It is powered by a fully custom engine. The engine compartment is a mechanic's dream—or nightmare. Gone are the greasy, dirty parts, but in their place are freshly painted ones. You have to be very careful not to chip the paint while working on it.*

*Not all sport truck owners are men. Stephanie Ruth is the proud owner of this 1986 Mazda B2000. She has made many of the modifications herself, with a little help and encouragement from her friend, Kris Hart. The seats she chose to use in her truck are from Auto Center, but she did the rest of the interior. Normally, thousands of dollars are paid to achieve a paint job of your choosing, but not so on this truck. The paint has been splattered or brushed on, and the outcome is quite attractive, showing creativity. Note the back of the mirror, wheels, door sides and so on.*

*Saleen Autosport of Anaheim, California, builds and markets sport truck conversions, be it for racing, like these two yellow conversions sponsored by Montgomery Ward and General Tire, or for fun, like the blue conversion on the following pages. Buying a conversion will save you the time and effort of finding all the individual components and then taking the time to assemble them, or pay someone to do the installation for you.*

GENERAL TIRE
Ultra Performance
TIRES
WHEELS
ACCESSORIES
5
GENERAL TIRE
GLENN HARRIS
Montgomery Ward
AutoExpress
GENERAL TIRE
KC
19
GENERAL TIRE
AuburnGear
AuburnGear
Ford Authorized Remanufacturers
PRO RACING
RANGER
Ford

SALEEN
Ranger
SALEEN